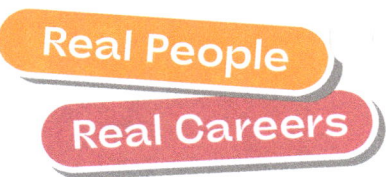

LIBRARIAN

© 2024 Julie Dascoli

All rights reserved. No part of this book may be reproduced or transmitted in any form or by any means, electronic or mechanical, including photocopying, recording or by any information storage and retrieval system, without prior permission in writing from the publisher.

Published in 2024 by Amba Press, Melbourne, Australia.
www.ambapress.com.au

Previously published in 2015 by Hawker Brownlow Education.
This edition replaces all previous editions.

ISBN: 9781923116801 (pbk)
ISBN: 9781923116818 (ebk)

A catalogue record for this book is available from the National Library of Australia.

LIBRARIAN

Written by Julie Dascoli

Photography by Laura Dascoli

Dear Reader,

Welcome to this volume of the *Real People Real Careers* series. I hope you'll enjoy learning about another exciting job people can do.

Before you read on, I'd like to say a few thank-yous to the people who helped to make this book possible.

Firstly, thank you to Laura Dascoli, who took the photographs you see in the book, and to Donna Dascoli, who provided initial editing and computer support services.

Secondly, my thanks to the staff and students in Years 4, 5 and 6 of the Mossgiel Park Primary School class of 2016 for their unwavering help and support.

And finally, I'm doubly grateful to Jessica, who generously gave up her time to help others learn about her profession — and to show them all the ways in which her job rules!

Happy reading!

Julie Dascoli

LIBRARIAN

My name is Jessica and I am a children's **Librarian**. I attended a state primary school, and then a Catholic secondary school in the Mt Dandenong Ranges, which is 47 kilometres from Melbourne City. During secondary school I did subjects like English, English Literature, Design and Technology, and Legal Studies.

My favourite subject was English Literature. My teacher was an actual story teller who used to tell us stories in between classes. This was very inspiring. I sought advice from all the people around me at my school, such as teachers and parents, regarding what I could do as a career.

All of them were of the opinion that I should be a teacher, but somehow it did not appeal to me. Soon it was the end of year twelve and I still had not decided what I wanted to do.

Once secondary school finished, I enrolled in a Bachelor of Arts specialising in **History** and **Literature**. This kind of course is a very general one that leaves one's options open. This course took three years to complete.

After I finished **university**, I answered an **advertisement** for a job as a **Customer Service Officer** in a library. I applied for the position and I was delighted to be invited for an **interview**. First there was a phone interview and then a face-to-face interview.

I was so excited to be told that I had the job, and asked to start straight away. After doing this job for six months, I was **promoted** to an **administration/management** position. I was enjoying working in the Library industry. I really enjoy helping people, problem solving and handling books every day. I felt inspired by the people that I worked with.

There was one man in particular who was a Librarian. He encouraged me to observe the way he worked, and allowed me to take part in story time. This is a service that is provided at many libraries. Children come in to the library and the librarian reads them a story and supervises activities themed around the story.

Before long, after watching the librarians do their job, I decided to **up-skill** and become a Librarian. I embarked on a **Master's degree** at university by **distance education.** This took another three years. Once this was complete I was eligible to apply for jobs as a librarian. I am now a **Youth Services Librarian** or **Children's Librarian.**

This job is very busy and exciting. My role includes so many different jobs; no day is ever the same. It can range from putting away the books that customers have returned, to helping customers find the books they are looking for, **coordinating** and performing story time and helping students find information. I also travel to kindergartens and schools to read to the children, and encourage their families to access the local libraries – and so much more.

Some of the tasks that I perform everyday are:

- → unlock the library when I arrive at work
- → turn on all of the equipment
- → clear the overnight returns chute
- → remove expired holds from the holds shelf
- → answer phone enquiries
- → help people find what they are looking for
- → help customers with photocopying, printing, scanning and computer use
- → check emails from **colleagues** and **suppliers**
- → collecting reserved books from the shelf for customers
- → tidy library in general and create fresh and interesting displays

My role includes so many different jobs; no day is ever the same.

REAL PEOPLE · REAL CAREERS

LIBRARIAN PAGE 7

Interesting facts about my job

- → It is free to join the library and to borrow books.
- → There are small fines if you don't bring your books back on time.
- → You can borrow as many books as you like at a time.
- → The library where I work is open from 10.00 a.m till 8.00 p.m. Monday till Thursday, 10.00 a.m. till 6.00 p.m. Fridays and 10.00 a.m till 4.00 p.m. Saturdays.
- → There are no only books on the library shelves; you can also borrow magazines, DVDs, eBooks, audio books and much more.
- → There are also thousands of resources that you can't borrow but can use in the library, such as magazines, newspapers and Internet access.
- → You can also access the library's website, and find a lot of free resources such as international and local newspapers, free tutors for students, language learning programs and games for children.
- → My favourite task is helping our customers find their next great read.
- → My least favourite task is shelving the books and ensuring they are all in perfect order.
- → I work seven hours per day in rotating shifts, including on evenings and weekends.

What I wear to work

Some libraries ask their staff to wear a uniform, however I do not have to at my current workplace. I wear neat casual attire, and closed-toe shoes. We work in air-conditioning so it doesn't change from winter to summer.

I wear neat casual attire, and closed-toe shoes

You can do my job if you:

- → enjoy helping people from all walks of life and of all ages
- → enjoy the company of children
- → like a job with plenty of variety
- → have a patient personality
- → have an enjoyment of books and movies
- → have a good understanding of technology
- → have a good sense of fun
- → are creative

The interactive nursery table has educational games for kids

This DAISY Player reads audiobooks for vision impaired people

Library visitors borrow, return and renew items at our self-service stations

Sometimes I dress up for a themed story time

Associated occupations

- → School librarian
- → Special librarian
- → Library technician
- → Customer Service Officer
- → Community engagement manager

Another happy customer

Barcode scanner to keep track of the library's possessions

LIBRARIAN

Postscript

Jessica continues to be the Librarian at a community library. She says this is her dream job. If she didn't have this job she would like to be a travel blogger, travelling the world writing about the world's 5-star restaurants and spas.

Glossary

Administration	The process of running a business or organisation. *Jessica's job includes administrative duties.*
Advertisement	A notice in a public medium promoting a product, service or event. *Jessica answered an advisement for the library Customer Service Officer's job.*
Attire	Clothing. *Jessica wears smart, casual attire to work each day.*
Blogger	A person who publishes a diary online for followers to read. *Jessica hopes to one day travel the world and be a blogger.*
Careers advisor	A person trained in giving advice to people about job possibilities. *Jessica obtained advice from many trusted people, including a careers advisor.*
Children's librarian	A librarian that specialises in children's literature. *Jessica became a Children's Librarian after working in libraries in other roles.*
Colleagues	The collective term for the people one works alongside. *Jessica checks her emails each day to communicate with her colleagues.*

Community engagement manager	The person who holds this position oversees programs that benefit the community.
Coordinating	To organise all elements to bring an event or situation to reality. *Jessica coordinates events in her role as Librarian.*
Customer Service Officer	The first point of contact one would meet when we go to the library. *Jessica was a Customer Service Officer before she did extra study to become a Librarian.*
Distance education	Studying at home either online or by correspondence. This allows a student to continue working and studying simultaneously. *Jessica studied a Master's degree by distance education and continued to work at the library.*
Expired holds	When a customer asks to have a book reserved for them but then fails to collect it. These books are held for a period of time and then are returned to the general collection as 'expired holds'. *Jessica and her colleagues return the expired holds to the shelves when the holding time lapses.*
History	The branch of knowledge dealing with past events. *History was one of the subjects Jessica specialised in at university.*

Interview
The process in which an employer who wants to hire a new staff member meets with a person who has applied for a job. The employer asks questions of the applicant, and the applicant can also ask questions to work out if they are the best person for the job. *Jessica attended an interview to apply for the job at the library.*

Library technician
An employee at a library who assists the librarian in the day-to-day tasks required to run it.

Literature
The collective word for all written works, i.e. poetry, novels, play scripts. *Jessica studied literature as one of her subjects at university.*

Management position
A position or job where the person will be in charge. *Jessica was promoted to a management position after six months of working at the library.*

Master's degree
A postgraduate course one can undertake as further study after an undergraduate degree. *Jessica undertook a Master's degree to gain a qualification as a Librarian.*

Overnight returns chute	A place where library customers can return their books after the library is closed. *Jessica and her colleagues empty the overnight returns chute and re-shelve the books every day.*
Pedometer	An instrument used to record how many steps a person undertakes, or the distance that has been travelled by foot. You can hire a pedometer from some libraries, along with many other things.
Promoted	To be raised to a position of higher duties and responsibility. *Jessica was promoted to an administration/management role.*
Suppliers	Companies who supply products and or services such as stationery or other goods an establishment may need to do their jobs. *Jessica communicates by email with suppliers.*

Other titles in this series

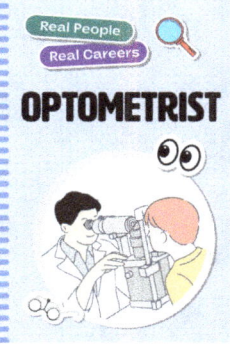

www.ingramcontent.com/pod-product-compliance
Lightning Source LLC
Chambersburg PA
CBHW070343120526
44590CB00017B/2999